The Definitive Guide to … Restaurant Magic

A guide to working as a restaurant magician.

By
Wayne Goodman

www.waynegoodman.co.uk

The Definitive Guide to ... Restaurant Magic

First paperback edition printed 2014 in the United Kingdom
A catalogue record for this book is available from the British Library.

ISBN 978-0-9928201-2-1

Published by Wayne Goodman Entertainments.
For more copies of this book please email:
wayne@waynegoodman.co.uk
Tel: (+44) 07726 190078
Designed and Set by Wayne Goodman Entertainments
Proof read and edited by: Dr Laura Cox
www.waynegoodman.co.uk
Printed in Great Britain

This book is dedicated to my beautiful daughter Charlee Goodman
&
Laura Cox, for her love and patience.

This book would not have been possible without the help of:
Stephen Leathwaite - Peter Nardi
Oliver Smith - Christian Fletcher - Mike Rose
Michael Murray - Chris Congreave - Chris Harding

Special Thanks go to:
Rodney James Piper – Joel Dickinson
Julie Carpenter - Matthew Ramsell

www.waynegoodman.co.uk

Wayne Goodman would like to thank the following people
for their support in the making of this book.

Elliot Phillips - Claire Marie Phillips - Lisa Robinson
Jasper Blakeley - Debra Quartermaine - Kelly Rumbol
Jamie Jigsaw - James Maidment

Introduction
by Stephen Leathwaite

Wayne is a character, a fearless comedy magician, who works in both close-up and cabaret.

At first glance Wayne is loud, audacious and is always cracking jokes, yet behind the laughs is a mind that is razor sharp. His knowledge is amazing, he has ideas that are realistic, real world strategies. Take just one idea from this book and implement it, you will see how much it changes the way you work, and the way you are seen to work.

At this time Wayne works for a large number of restaurants in a residency capacity, earning a steady and decent wage every month before his private events, weddings and trade shows.

With 25 years in the business, and a phone book that resembles a who's who of the restaurant business, when Wayne starts talking, you will want to listen, as he knows more about the business of restaurant magic than most people will ever know.

When Wayne and I did the "Road Mage Podcast", I learnt a lot from listening to him speak. It was strange, I already knew some of the things he would say, but the way that Wayne was using these simple techniques, I knew they would yield strong responses.

After Wayne had finished the rough draft of this book, he sent it to me to have a read through. I looked at it and thought "It isn't a big book", but after I finished reading it, I felt alive and I started working on new business cards and some brochures.

If you want to know the business side of getting long-term

repeat gigs, then look no further than this book, it really is a gold mine, are you ready to make it work for you.

I know Wayne has decided to write a series of books, covering almost every aspect of the work we do, stage, close-up, etc. I know the books will be amazing, and this is the perfect start to that collection.

Finally I want to add, that I know a lot of you will be thinking, "Yeah, Wayne and Stephen are great mates, of course he is going to say it is a great book". This is true, we are great mates, but after reading the book, I knew it was something I would be proud to put my name to.

Trust me, read and implement, you will not be disappointed.

Stephen Leathwaite

Flatcap Productions.

Forward.

In 2012 I recorded a podcast with Stephen Leathwaite called "The Road Mage Podcast".

We discussed many subjects on the podcast, but no other subject evoked so many questions than ideas for getting restaurant residency work.

How do I get the job?
How much should I charge?
How does it differ from a normal gig?

The biggest response I got though was people saying I should put all the information into a book, and after two years and a lot of writing and rewriting you now hold the result.

I wanted to avoid the kind of book that is packed with filler - pages upon pages of words with no value. This may not be a big book, but the pages are jam-packed with solid principles and workable ideas.

Over the last 10 years I have made a healthy and very steady income from regular work in the restaurant market.

During times when the regular gigs, weddings, trade shows and parties are a little slow, I am still earning proper money and generating contacts.

A lot of the ideas in this book are not exclusive to residencies, you can apply them to your normal gigs too.

Working in restaurants is a lot of fun, you get to know the staff and the regulars, you build contacts and work out new material.

All the information in this book has been tried and tested over many years, I hope you will enjoy reading it and then have a lot of enjoyment from going out and doing it.

Best wishes

Wayne Goodman
2014

Working in Restaurants.

Are you the kind of performer who can work in a restaurant / residency style arena?

This is very important as your performance style may not suit certain elements of the environment you are now looking at.

Example: A friend of mine works a lot behind a table. He performs tricks based around using the table (out of this world, 4 ace assemblies, etc). This works great for him at house parties; however, he would really struggle in a busy restaurant - you have to consider the waiting staff carrying trays of hot and cold drinks, the food being brought to the table and being cleared away. I have heard of some magicians that carry their own small table with them around the restaurant, I personally would never even consider this for the restaurants I work in. However if it works for them...

Does your act allow for the constraints of this kind of performance?

Can you repeat, repeat, repeat, and then be prepared when you see the same people the next week/month/whenever? Can you perform under almost any angle and with other tables watching? Do you have the repertoire that allows you to switch routines half-way through the evening? Thread set ups are pretty much out of the question, most venues will not allow fire or flash products and if they do you will have to arrange a risk assessment.

What kind of audience do you want to be working for?

This will completely direct where you will look for work: for example, there is no point looking at Frankie and Benny's if you cannot stand working with families or children.

Some restaurants dictate the kind of customers they get, you will not find many families in a high-end French bistro, but you will in a big chain pizza/Italian/American restaurant.

Do you understand the logistical and financial differences between residencies and one-off gigs?

This is a big question and will be covered in more detail later on; however, you need to make a decision regarding choosing a specific time of the week to dedicate to one venue, regardless of other shows coming in. Once you are established in the venue you can organise cover when you have other work, but I would advise against this in the early days - you do not want to lose the gig to someone else because you are never there.

So now you have decided that you are able and willing to do this kind of work, it is time to actually get into a restaurant and show just how good you are. Unless you are very lucky and hit it straight off, the process can take some time. You will need what I call the 3 P's, and you will need a lot of all three:

Passion - Patience - Publicity

The Restaurants.

First things first, right now you should open up google and type in these immortal, world-changing words:

"Restaurants in (your) area"

Now visit all these pages and directories and start building a database of managers names, phone numbers, emails, etc.

Large chain restaurants can be harder to get into, but offer more stability, and like most big businesses they are all connected.

I have included below a list of some of my major clients, and a list of the companies they own. Use this information wisely, do not approach every venue in the company. A better way is to work your way into one, then use this connection to work with the sister companies. If you approach all the restaurants at the same time, it is possible that they will all end up at the same person, you will go from possible supplier to spam in less time than it takes to say, "No thanks".

Here is the list of companies I work with on a regular basis:

The Restaurant Group (TRG) owns a number of high street food chains, and is a major player in the restaurant game.

www.trgplc.com/

Frankie & Benny's

Little Frankie's

Chiquito's

Garfunkel's

Coast to Coast

FS Filling Station

Bluebeckers

Brunning & Price

Home Counties Pub restaurants

Whitbread is another group to look at:

www.whitbread.co.uk

Premier Inn

Table Table

Costa Coffee

Beefeater

Taybarns

Brewers Fayre

The Montaz group is a restaurant chain in my home town of Newmarket; they have 5 restaurants within a 20 mile area

www.montaz.co.uk

Brinker International has a smaller number of brands, but have a vast number of restaurants around the USA and UK:

www.brinker.com

Chilli's

Maggiano's

Gondola Holdings owns and runs a few major chains that you will find in most towns and especially near cinema complexes:

www.gondolaholdings.com

Zizzi

ASK Italian

Pizza Express

Milano (the Pizza Express brand in Ireland)

Byron

Kettner's

GREENE KING
BURY ST EDMUNDS

Green King is a major company in the restaurant industry:

www.greeneking.co.uk

Hungry Horse

Old English Inn's

Eating Inn

Loch Fyne Seafood Grill

Green King Pubs

Belhaven Pubs and Restaurants

Plus you have Pizza Hut, Prezzo and many more similar style restaurants.

(All information is correct at time of writing)

When a manager leaves one of these restaurants, it is normally to go to another venue in the same chain or to another company altogether - this can be very beneficial to you: I was introduced to three major corporations because the manager moved and moved again.

Getting The Gig.

I am fortunate that at this stage in my career, mainly through hard work, I now have restaurants approaching me. However, in the early days you will need to do the cold calling, letter/email writing and the chasing.

You will need to do some research and get as much information as you can. You may have been booked to perform at the venue, in which case you're ahead of the game here, however a little extra research goes a long way:

How many tables/covers a night?

How busy does the venue get?

Which days are busy and which are quiet?

Is it a family restaurant or is it mostly just adults?

How expensive is it to eat there?

What is the average cost of a meal for a family?

Do they currently have entertainment in the venue?

If they do have other entertainment, if so what is it?

Do they have a bar area?

During the busiest times how long is the wait for a table?

Once you have all this information, you will need to decide how you want to approach the establishment.

There are a number of ways you can do this, some are quite direct, others more subtle. I will list a few below, but whatever you choose to do, you need to make sure it fits your style and personality. I heard of one young performer who went in to a restaurant all guns blazing, the manager loved his passion but after a few weeks, found he was unable to maintain the high energy needed, and quickly faded, his energy levels dropped and he was soon gone from the restaurant.

Go into the venue for a meal or drink - have a chat with the bar staff, get some information and then ask to speak to the manager/owner.

Write to the venue and deliver the letter by hand – this could lead to an impromptu meeting, so make sure you go to the restaurant prepared.

Email the venue.

Go into the venue for a meal or drink

If you are looking at a big chain like Nando's or Chiquito's then this is probably your best option. The management have decision making authority, and sometimes they have a budget for entertainment and can make a decision, if not immediately, then quite quickly. For smaller, independent venues the owner (who will be the decision maker) may not be around during the evening and would not be there to witness what you do, however if you impress the manager then that may grease the wheels towards meeting the owner.

Write to the venue and deliver the letter by hand

Email is great, but it is very easy for your mail to get lost in the junk mail, and forget asking for a read-receipt - this will just wind the manager up. Get some nice paper, and write them a letter. By all means do this on the computer and print it off, but use decent paper, put your letter in a matching envelope and address it properly - even though you will deliver by hand, it adds a touch of elegance. First impressions really do count, so make sure you provide the best. Time your arrival so that the manager/owner is there but also when there will be customers around. You don't want it to be really busy, but for there to be enough people to show what you can do without being in the way or causing harassment. For this approach I would also suggest taking along an information package, what some may call a press kit. This will include all the publicity material that you think is relevant to the venue, if you choose to do this via email then links to web pages and other relevant information should be included. In my information kit I would include a brochure, postcard and business card alongside the personalised letter to the venue.

Email the venue

The content of your email will be very similar to that described for a hand-delivered letter. However, the main difference between this and going in person is that it is much easier to click an email back to say "No Thanks" or even ignore it completely. If you do decide to use this approach, keep the email short and to the point; provide details of the service you are offering and links to your website and any promotional videos, etc.

With all of the approaches mentioned above you need to make sure you are talking to the right person. The bar manager may be the nicest person in the world, but if they do not have the decision making ability then **at this point** you are talking to the wrong person.

You must also be wary of being taken for a ride.

In this case they will ask you to come in on a particular night, with the promise of more work and then just use and reject you

They get a free night's entertainment on a busy night, and you get nothing apart from a night's work for no fee. Maintaining control of the decisions is important, if they offer you a night they know will be busy because they have a big party coming in will normally start alarm bells ringing: try and arrange your demonstration for a night when you know they will be busy with normal customers and not when the venue has been reserved for a single group.

Reasons They Should Book You.

For this section I spoke to one of the managers I work for, and asked him what it means to him to have me in the restaurant. His answers show how the venue managers see what you do:

- The customer gets more from their visit to the restaurant,
  this positive experience will be told to others and will generate more income to the restaurant.
- Additional attention for the customers - something that every manager knows will encourage new and repeat business and increase tips.
- Makes the dining experience more pleasurable.
- Keeps attention away from any delays.
- Enhances the reputation of the restaurant.
- Helps with waiting times, at the tables (while servers are
  busy elsewhere) and in the bar area (while guests are waiting for a table).

I decided to put together some FAQs that I have had from interested managers, and my answers to these questions.

Is magic right for my venue?

Every restaurant is different, and each requires a different approach. With over 25 years in the business and working for many different restaurants, I can look at the venue and evaluate the best way to make the performances a success. I will complement the service you give, and add to the excellent team you already have working here.

Can magic make a difference to the customer's experience?

Yes it can, simple as that. Every table will experience moments of wonder, comedy and amazing magic. Whether they are having a celebration, a birthday meal, marking an anniversary or a family dinner out, all will feel that they have had special attention and that their meal out has been enhanced. Regulars in the venue will see something different every time they come, and will be the first to let you know just how much the other customers enjoy it.

Will this interfere with the running of the restaurant?

Absolutely not. In fact it will be an asset - if there is a delay in the kitchen or waiting time for a table to become available, I will help by filling this dead time to the point that most customers will not even realise there has been a delay.

Remember these points when meeting with the management:
- Enjoy the meeting.
- Keep it professional but make sure to show you have a fun personality.
- Focus on what you are there to do. Keep to the point and do not waffle.
- Remember the details of what you are offering. There is nothing wrong with having notes in a file.
- Stay calm, the manager WILL ask questions: be prepared, PAUSE, think, then answer.
- Do not be scared to say "I don't know". Do not start making up information or make promises you will not be able to deliver on.
- The manager is a busy person: ensure the meeting has a meaning.
- Do some magic, but do not turn the meeting into a show. Remember this is a business meeting.

- End the meeting on a positive.
- The meeting may not end with a decision, so remind the manager you **will** follow up within 7 days.
- Enjoy the meeting.

I know the first and last points are the same, and it was done on purpose to remind you to enjoy it. The meeting is not life or death, you are not committing espionage, so… enjoy it, stay calm, be yourself and make an impression.

What to do when you visit.

These suggestions could well lead to you getting the gig:

- Chat to the regulars at the bar or any off-duty staff, they will be made up that you made time for them and will have the ear of the manager long after you have left the venue.

- When you do get to perform for the manager/owner, make sure the effect you do is appropriate and outstanding. This should be something that will blow them away and leave them thinking about you for the rest of the day. If you can do a trick that leaves them with a souvenir then so much the better.

- If you are going to offer a free night, do it on your terms: suggest nights that you know they will be busy, but maintain control over when you are available.

- Make sure you know the manager's name and get their business card - this way you have direct contact details for them.

- Show an interest in their business: ask questions about when and how busy it gets.

What NOT to do when you visit.

- If you have an arranged time, **DO NOT** be late. This is a major turn-off to any potential booker, and is really disrespectful. Better to be an hour early and sit in your car than 1 minute late.

- **DO NOT** turn up dressed as a magician, complete with a full array of effects. Be smartly dressed and well presented but I would avoid any magic badges or card ties. Lurid waistcoats and silly hats also will count against you. The manager/owner is a business person and this is a business meeting not a show. If you wear a costume whilst working bring in photos, do not wear the costume to the meeting.

- **DO NOT** perform too many tricks. "**Less is more**" is the message here: keep them wanting more and show you know what you are doing. Too much and you become a bore, or even worse an inconvenience. Food and drink are the main money pullers, not the magician: the message you need to convey is as an asset, not an attention-seeking show-off.

- **DO NOT** push your luck or their patience. Do what you came to do, but remember the manager/owner is a busy person. Be polite and prepared (know your subject) but do not expect them to hang around when the meeting is over.

- **DO NOT** bring up the subject of fees or money. Let them do the chasing and ask the questions.

- **DO NOT** be scared to ask for more time on the money front. Say you will prepare a package that will offer your service at an attractive price that is complementary to the standards of the restaurant.

The Fee.

Some magicians will tell you they refuse to leave the house for less than £1,000, they never have a bad show, and are normally multi-award winning, international magicians.

Most restaurants will not be able to pay your normal show fee on a regular basis, so the first thing is to accept that you will be working for less money; however, this does not mean you will be working for less. One of my major residencies has generated a vast volume of work for me, including a number of high-end clients, trade shows and loyal customers who book me year after year.

I generally get paid between £100 and £250 for my residencies. I work (once a month) for a small (20 seater) Indian restaurant which is 100 yards from my home: they give me £100 for 2 hours on a TUESDAY night (when I am not overbooked with weekend or corporate gigs), plus I normally get a meal to bring home for me and my other half.

Another one of my venues pays me £250 twice a month, to perform on a Sunday afternoon 12.00pm – 3pm during their very busy Sunday lunchtime slot.

You need to look at each restaurant on its individual merits and base your fee accordingly.

A large chain restaurant with 40 tables (seating approximately 200 people) with an average £90 per table of 4 (not including drinks), with 2 sittings per evening (6.30pm – 11pm), will generate approximately £7,200.

compared to:

A small independent with 10 tables (seating approximately 40 people) with an average £80 per table of 4 (not including drinks), with 2 sittings per evening (6.30pm – 10pm), will generate approximately £1,600.

There appears to be a huge big difference in income and, you might suppose, entertainment budget; however, this is not the whole picture. Let's compare two of my long term residencies [all figures correct at time of writing (January 2014)]:

The large chain restaurant:

Is open all day - meaning a bigger revenue not just from food but also drinks, especially as the venue has a large bar area.

This restaurant has a minimum daily target of £18,000 for Monday – Thursday, £40,000 for Friday and Saturday, and £25,000 for Sunday; targets are broken down into four sections: Breakfast – Lunch – Dinner - Drinks

However, this restaurant also has big expenses: lots of staff both on the floor and in the kitchens, in addition to back up staff and management; the venue is large and located in a popular complex, so building costs will be higher as will amenities and local taxes.

Being part of a chain made it harder to get into, I had to convince the manager, he had to convince the area manager, and she had to get clearance from head office.

Now let's compare this to the other end of the scale:

The small, independent Indian restaurant:

This restaurant opens later in the day (6pm), and has a minimum daily target of £1,000 for Sunday – Thursday and £1,800 for Friday and Saturday.

There is no bar area, so there is not a target for sales on extra drinks; however, it does sell a few extra drinks to people waiting to collect take-a-ways.

Staff numbers are low: two people in the kitchen plus three waiters on the floor, including one manager (normally the owner).

This restaurant is not part of a chain, so I was able to meet with the higher echelons almost straight away, make my presentation directly to the decision makers and get the booking confirmed almost immediately.

This is still only the tip of the iceberg, but a small look at the venues should make you think more about your fee and how you need to take into account your own extras, Public Liability Insurance, petrol, Tax, and any other costs.

How much you charge not only reflects how much you think you are worth, but also speaks volumes to the manager about how serious you are about what you are proposing.

When it comes to the negotiations don't be afraid to let the management know how much you would charge for a Wedding or corporate event so they realise what a good deal they are getting by booking you on a regular basis.

"When it comes to how much this is going to cost, and to put it into perspective, if you wanted to book me for a 2 hour session doing table magic, you would pay in the region of £350 - £450. However, as you are interested in booking me on a regular basis, we can bring that price down to a figure that fits both our budgets."

This simple sentence tells the manager that you are actually worth a lot more than he will be paying for, and that you want to make a serious commitment to the venue.

You may be inclined to add the word "Right" to the last part and say

"We can bring that price RIGHT down to a figure that fits both our budgets".

This is a mistake, it may imply that the fee you want is actually much lower than it is, thus misleading the negotiations towards a line much lower than you want to accept.

You will need to decide what you're happy to work for, in the same way you do when you work for a birthday, dinner, trade show, etc.

You must also be ready to deal with any negotiations with the management.

Try to be as transparent as possible, the above scenario tells the manager what your normal price is, and what you are willing to lower it to - you have moved the goal posts, now he needs to meet you at price that's right for you both. They will probably try and get you to lower your price further - this is basic negotiation practice in any line of work; however, you do not want to lower the price too much: you must maintain a level of control over what is being agreed.

I have encountered this situation many times: you are at the point of signing the contracts, with an agreed-upon price, when the manager demands a steep discount or the deal is off.

"My area manager wants to make the price 25% lower or we just cannot make it work"

What is actually happening here is the manager wants to know that he has definitely got the best price. The worst thing you can do is give in to this, otherwise the manager will wonder if they can get more money off next month to keep you there.

The correct way to deal with this is simple, rather than lower the price, change the deal.

"Sorry, the price I've offered is the best price I can do. However, if you are really serious about the service I provide but want to lower the price, maybe we can shorten the session to match the price you want to pay".

When I have had to say this, the manager has always backed down and said that he would speak to his manager and they would find a way to make it work - I doubt the area manager had ever made such a request.

The manager will see you are offering the best price, and that you will only lower price if the duration is lowered. They will want to get their money's worth from you, so a shorter session, even for less money is a loss for them.

Stand your ground and be clever. You do not need to be ruthless, but you do need to show you know and understand your own business, as well as understanding their business.

The Follow Up.

You have written letters, sent emails and visited the restaurant.

What do you do now? How do you follow up? What happens if they say the dreaded NO?

Some managers/owners will make a decision on the spot: you are either hired or not. Some will require some time to think about it, or will need to get an area manager to sign off on it.

The follow up is in some ways the hardest part of the process, mainly because it is a waiting game. Once you have finished with the meeting, how long do you wait before following up with the manager?

There are a couple of ways to eliminate the waiting period, for instance at the end of the face-to-face meeting I normally mention that I will drop them an email in the next few days, as a professional courtesy. This means I will not appear pushy or too keen when I email 4 - 5 days later.

Normally you do not want to wait more than 7 - 8 days before following up, any longer and you will be forgotten and you will be back to square one. The ideal follow up time is 4 - 5 days later, this gives the face-to-face meeting some time to sink in, it also means the manager will have worked a couple of shifts and will have imagined what you being there would do for the venue.

A typical follow up letter would look something like this:

Dear "Name of manager"

I really enjoyed visiting you last week at "Name of restaurant" and meeting with yourself, your staff and customers. I hope you got some great feedback from the demonstration and can see that I can be a great asset to the restaurant. Through the use of mutual promotion via my website, your website and social media outlets I believe we can create a regular event that will increase customers for the restaurant and offer a service that is unique.

I look forward to hearing from you soon

Wayne Goodman
The Restaurant Magician
www.waynegoodman.co.uk

This kind of letter is simple, direct and promotes the service and potential increase in customers and therefore profit to the company.

The manager may ask for some more time as it's a busy period and s/he has not had a chance to review it all yet, or has not had a chance to speak to the area manager, etc: this is not a rejection, and you should respond accordingly: "No problem, I understand you're busy. Shall I give you a call next week, on Tuesday maybe?".

Do not be too pushy but let them know you are serious about working for them, whilst giving them space to make a decision.

YAY OR NAY

The waiting is done, the manager has called or emailed and it's either **YAY or NAY:**

If it is YAY, then well done, the hard work and waiting has paid off, time to move on further into the book.

If it is NAY, do not take it as a knock-back: they have SERIOUSLY considered you; maybe the company is reducing expenses as a run up to something, and you just had bad timing. It could have been any of a hundred reasons but you do not need to focus on that, for you the main focus must now be to move forward and carry on. Remember, they may have said no, but they have not said you should not try again. I'm not saying you should try again straight away, but you should not give up altogether.

I have a number of restaurants who have said no to booking me, that I still pop into, have a drink or a meal, keep an eye on the management and get known by the staff. This is useful as you get to know the main players in the venue, and if the situation changes you are known to be around and in their minds for a try out. Also one of the staff may be promoted and move to another venue and want to use you there, or if it is the manager leaving they may have more freedom at their new restaurant and book you for there. Alternatively, if you believe the decision was down to the old manager's personal opinions, they may be replaced by a new manager who may be more inclined to have you in the restaurant: by befriending the staff they will also push you to the new manager.

Making friends and building bridges is one of the most important aspects of any business, especially entertainment.

Contracts.

Once the agreements are completed you will need to send the management a contract package.

This will generally include:

1) The contract agreement.
2) A copy of your PLI Certificate.
3) The terms and conditions of your contract: also known as the Rider.
4) Payment Details and Agreements.

Depending on the company I am working for, I normally have to invoice them at the end of the month for the total amount. Some companies may ask you to invoice after each session though, and some may even pay you cash at the end of the evening.

The contract should be a recurring contract that states "Repeat sessions as agreed", this negates the need to send a new contract every time - their accounts department will deal with the invoices each month.

Get to know the key people, learn the names and positions of the people who are going to be paying you. If you have any problems you can go directly to the right people and get it sorted out quickly.

The main contract should include all the details that you agree with the management.

This should include:

- Length of each session (e.g.: 3 hours including 2x 5 minute breaks).
- Times of each session (e.g.: 5pm-8pm every first and third Thursday of the month).
- Agreed Fee.
- Any specialist agreements you have made, such as staff parking, food and drinks included, etc.

The contract should look professional and if you do not have confidence in writing one yourself then you can always ask someone in the business, copy mine below, look online for contract writers, or ask someone in the legal community.

Below is a copy of one of my contracts.

The terms and conditions have been omitted as each company would receive a custom rider that is relevant to my requirements from that company. There is no point asking for a staff car parking space if there is no staff car parking.

ENTERTAINMENTS

Wayne Goodman

www.waynegoodman.co.uk

Company Registration Number - 2269802

CONTRACT AND INVOICE NUMBER:

Whilst every reasonable safeguard is assured, Wayne Goodman Entertainments will not be held responsible for any breach of contract by the Engager or by the Artiste.

This document reflects the legally binding verbal agreement already made.

Please note that failure to sign and return the contract IS NOT sufficient to cancel the agreement

BETWEEN (THE ENGAGER):

CONTACT NUMBER: AND (THE ARTISTE): Wayne Goodman

Whereby the Engager engages the Artiste and the Artiste accepts the engagement to present/appear as known as scheduled below

DATE OF ENGAGEMENT(S):

VENUE: TIMES:

TYPE OF SHOW:

TOTAL FEE: £

PAYMENT METHOD:

(Fee) to be paid within 30 days via bank transfer to (Bank Details).

ADDITIONAL CLAUSES: Soft drinks whilst working, Staff Car Parking space and Access to staff area.

(ANY ATTACHED SCHEDULE OR CONTRACT RIDER FORMS AN INTEGRAL PART OF THIS AGREEMENT)

I the undersigned acknowledge that I have read the above contract together with any Rider and the terms and conditions.

Contacts.

The people you meet and the contacts you make are possibly the most important assets you will acquire.

My first residency was for a Frankie & Benny's: a large Italian/American Chain restaurant owned and run by "The Restaurant Group".

It's not what you know, it's who you know.

The manager when I started there was a man named Kevin. This man has forgotten more about the running of a restaurant than I will ever know. We worked together for approximately 18 months before he left to run a restaurant for a different company. When he left he took with him four members of staff (including two managers) to work at the new restaurant, he also booked me to do his opening night, and then to work regularly in the new restaurant afterwards.

Since that occasion, Kevin has moved three times and each time he started somewhere new, I was there for the opening night, followed by regular slots afterwards. Kevin is now a senior manager in a large company and oversees the running of a number of venues, all of which I have regular work in.

Not only have I had all these bookings from Kevin, but one of the managers he took with him to the new venue was a young lady named Kelly; when she left the second company to work for a different restaurant chain, guess who she took along to opening night to make an impression? That's right, yours truly. We have since negotiated a contract for regular work there too.

So I took one venue, I worked hard and made sure the right people heard positive feedback, I formed a good relationship with the staff and management and I got additional venues and increased my revenue. I also gained many contacts at the new venues and also giving out business cards whilst working.

The contacts that you make can mould and shape your future career. You never know the directions that people will take in their careers, you could work with a waitress in a small independent restaurant who ends up running a major corporation, booking you year after year for multiple events and dinners. I have made such connections.

The First Night.

So we are finally here, and the first night is upon us! For the first couple of sessions, the residency is no different from a normal gig.

It will not be until the 3rd or 4th session, when you have repeat customers and have exhausted all your effects with the regulars that you start to feel the pattern enclosing around you. Do not be tempted to rush in with all your best material: have good material on you, but pace yourself, hopefully you are in for a long run, and you do not want to wear yourself down.

Be Early:

Get to the venue early and look round the seating plan, find out if there are many reservations, and where the big groups will be sat. Work out when it will get busy and when you will need to switch styles from fast paced to slow paced.

If you have a large number of tables being filled at 8pm, then 7.50pm maybe a good time to plan a break and restock any cards or other effects so that you do not need to do this when the restaurant is busy.

Speak to the floor staff:

Let them know that you are there to complement the service and if they have any problem customers or delays that you can be utilised to diffuse the situation or fill the gap.

Be seen:

If the venue is quiet do not hide out the back or in the staff area (unless the manager asks you to go through and entertain the staff).

Learn names:

Learn the names of everyone, from the cleaners to the managers, and remember you are all important and all part of a team.

Learn the numbers:

Every table has a number, so if a member of the floor staff says "Can you go to table 47" you know exactly where you are headed.

First impressions really do matter:

Choose the first table wisely, make an impact and let everyone know you are there for a reason. The first night will be the first chance for the manager see if you can live up to the promises you have sold them.

Most of all have fun and do some great magic.

Approaching The Table.

This is a subject that is always cropping up.
What is the best way to approach the table?
How do you introduce yourself to the people at the table?
What group is the best group to approach first?

First of all let's look at how NOT to approach a table…

These two approaches are best avoided:

"Excuse me, did you drop this RED pen knife?"
(Then start some convoluted colour changing knife routine)

"Sorry sir, did you ask for a spare spoon?"
(Then bend the spoon)

Also I would recommend not pushing your magic onto the customers without first asking permission, fire wallets and flash effects are classic examples of this. Be careful not to ask the customers whether they would like to see some magic only to start before they can reply.

My motto is: "Do not start your set with an effect to get their attention, rather start with an introduction to get their respect".

"Good evening Ladies and Gentlemen. My name is Wayne and I am the magician here tonight. I have been booked by the restaurant to perform around the tables. Do you mind if I join you for a few minutes?"

Wow - nothing ground breaking, no witty banter, no clever lines or cheesy tricks. This approach has worked for me, for more years than I can remember: it's simple, and it works. You should never underestimate the power of simplicity.

I have tried many different ways of approaching the tables, including comedic methods and clever speeches, however the above approach works for me 99% of the time. Do remember that your choice of first table will make a huge impact on how other tables see you, as will your personality in the venue and how you interact with other staff members.

Who is best to perform to first.

Choosing your first table is a very important decision.

Ideally you want a table either mixed with young people or a family with older children who will respond in a positive manner. The minimum you want from the table is a round of applause, this lets other customers know who you are and what you are doing.

You want to avoid couples and small children. Couples or quiet tables are no good, you will perform and get little or no reaction and after you leave them, you're back to square one looking for a lively table to make your presence known. Families with small children are also best avoided to begin with, I always have tricks on me that are suitable for kids but

I do not want to become the kid's magician in the restaurant.

I will add here, that I am not saying that you should not work for these groups of people, just that these tables are not the ideal way to start the session. You want to make an impression and let the whole room know who you are, and why you are there. A good cheer or round of applause sets this up nicely.

Remember these people are here to eat, they have not come to see you - you are not the main attraction. You need to be polite and courteous, remember that once the interest has been built it will be easier to be accepted at the other tables.

If they say no:
This is going to happen, you are going to be rejected, but do not take it personally. Some people will not want to be entertained, they may have had a rough day at work, be having family issues, they may just want to chat or be left alone.

The best way to handle this crushing blow is to smile, be polite and leave the table.

My normal line of patter would be:

Customer: "*No thanks, I am not interested*".

Me: "*No problems, I am working here till 8pm so if you change your mind, just let me know or ask the waiter and I will come back over. Enjoy your meal and thanks for coming to "Name of Restaurant".*"

As I leave, I place a business card on the table and move onto the next table I plan on working.

If I am rejected from a table, I would avoid going to another table in direct proximity to the one I have just been turned away from. You do not want to start a chain reaction of "*NO*", so I would head to another section and start again.

A lot of performers have asked me the best way to deal with this rejection, and a lot of people who are new to this kind of work worry about the thought of being turned away. Their main fear is that this rejection means they are not very good or that they have somehow failed. This could not be further from the truth, when the waiter asks if the customer would like a dessert, if they say no, the waiter does not get upset or feel like he has failed. Instead he says "no problem" and carries on.

Working The Table.

So you have approached the table and they have said "Yes", now they are all sat, silent and waiting, watching you with anticipation and excitement. What wonders are you about to show them? Well, get on with it!

If you are a regular gig performer, then this should be no problem, you will know which effects grab applause, and which tricks get good reactions.

However, if you have never performed, or never in this environment, you may wonder what effects are going to amaze and astound.

Every magician is different, and you will have a style of your own - you will have practised some effects and made up a short routine. Is it good enough? What tricks do the professionals use?

What tricks do I perform:

When I am working I will have a number of effects on me; however, I want them to be co-ordinated and also complement each other.

I generally have 3 different sets on me at any time.

A)

My own pick a card routine leading into and ending with my own effect "Look Sharp".

Bill Switch (sometimes using Gregory Wilson's Legal Tender to finish with).

Blind Date by Stephen Leathwaite.

B)

Child's Play by Chris Congrieve.

Exact Change By Gregory Wilson.

My own "Film Reading" routine using the amazing Stealth Assassin (www.alakazam.co.uk).

I also carry a normal pack of cards on me to perform multiple routines and extras with if I want to fill time, or do not feel like I have enough time to do a set routine before I will need to leave the table.

If there are children on the table I will do:

Sponge Ball routine, I use either the simple routine you get with most sets or the excellent David Stone routine off his DVD set (you may also look at sponge rabbits, etc).

Thumb Tip and silk for a simple vanish. Sometimes I will make the silk reappear in the sleeve of the child. To do this, have the child hold out their arm and as you hold the wrist slip your thumb into the end of the sleeve, holding the thumb tip through the material; with your other hand you can extract the silk, then look into the sleeve and ask "is there anything else? Any rabbits?" and extract the tip with your thumb.

A simple coin magic, using a borrowed 50p if possible. I do some simple manipulation then the muscle pass to get a wow and then give the child the coin to keep. Normally getting a laugh from any adults, especially is the coin is taken off an adult who is not the child's parent.

Once I had compiled this list I also asked a few other full time performers to add their own sets.

I would like to thank Stephen Leathwaite, Christian Fletcher, Julie Carpenter and Matthew Ramsell for helping me with this section.

Stephen Leathwaite

"I use a lot of material but these are most regular effects:

- Slop shuffle
- Hotshot cut by Daryl: The encyclopedia of card slights volume 8
- Specs fx
- The box by Mark Southworth
- Look Sharp by Wayne Goodman (www.alakazam.co.uk)
- Disposable by Stephen Leathwaite: Lethal Weapons DVD
- The butterfly pass by Stephen Leathwaite: Butterfly pass project DVD
- For walk around I always have rubber bands on me, and I use effects from the Dan Harlan rubber band magic DVD sets."

For more details on Stephen's own material check out www.flatcapmagicshop.co.uk

Christian Fletcher

- Bill Switch
- Ambitious Card
- 3 Card Monte
- Bill in Kiwi
- Metal Bending (Morgan Streblers Liquid Metal)
- Ring Flight Revolution by Dave Bonsall (www.propdog.co.uk)

Julie Carpenter

- Pavels Jumping Knot
- Unequal Ropes
- Chicago Opener
- Hopping Halves

Matthew Ramsell

- Ambitious Card
- Omni Deck
- To The Max
- Chaotic Sponge Balls
- Fly-drive

• How long should I stay at the table?

This will depend on when you are at the table, and how much you know from the floor staff. Every time I am in a restaurant, I ask what the average wait time is from order to table, this will depend on other factors, including:

• How busy is the restaurant?

If the restaurant is busy then food may take a little longer to come out, this will also be affected by what style of restaurant you are working in. A Chinese or Indian restaurant that cooks big pans of food will supply the food a lot quicker than a restaurant that is cooking individual dishes to order.

• How big is the group of people on the table?

A bigger group is another cause for delay, be prepared for a longer set if required to fill this gap.

- **At what stage of their meal are they at?**

If the customers have just ordered their food then you can expect the food to be on the way and you will know roughly how long that is, as you will have spoken to the floor staff earlier. If, however, you get to the table at the end of their meal, then as long as there are not others waiting for this table, then you may have a little longer to be here. I find the end of the meal tables very informal and relaxed and it is in these situations that I may try out new material for the first time.

- **What happens if the food arrives and I am half way through a trick?**

Then finish, and move on. You can always go back later and if the effect allows then do it again. If the client asks you to stay and finish the effect, then do so, but do not be in the way and do not drop anything in the food. I have seen it happen, not to me, but I have seen it.

Leaving The Table or Leaving An Impression?

When I have finished my set and I am about to leave the table, I want to make sure that I am leaving on a positive note.

There are a couple of things that are going through my mind as I do this. If I want them to have had a good time, I need to know:

- Have I left them happy, after enjoying a memorable experience?
- Have I left them wanting more?
- Have I left business cards/postcards on the table?

I always let the table know that I am working for the evening and if they wish to see some more, then to give me a wave or stop me when I am walking around.

I always thank the customer for coming to the restaurant at the end of my set.

Remember, you are part of the staff even though you are independent of the restaurant, so it is always good to remind them you are glad they came out.

I personally do not like accepting tips when I am working. I would rather the money go to the floor staff, my main reason for this is that it keeps me in the waiting staff's good books. One way to side step this, so as not to offend the person offering, is to say that all tips are pooled so if they would like to leave a tip at the end of their meal that would be great. Sometimes however I do accept tips, and I have included a chapter on accepting tips, and ways to get more tips elsewhere in the book.

For me I would rather a round of applause and/or a word to the manager when they leave, which has a lot more value to me than a few coins in my pocket.

Remember customers and their names, so when they are leaving the restaurant you can pass by and thank them again.
"Cheers for coming see you again next time" is great. However, if you say "Thanks for coming tonight James, I look forward to seeing you and Sarah again soon" it carries a lot more power with the customer. Everyone loves to feel special and remembering their name leaves a lasting impression.

Remember:

- Leave them wanting more.
- Leave a positive impression of both the venue and of yourself.
- Leave some form of publicity material.

Staff Assistance.

The floor staff can be an amazing help. Simple actions can result in great responses; however, this can be a slow process and will depend on your relationship with the waiting staff and maître de or host/hostess.

With a good team behind you, the hardest part of our job (getting accepted by the table) can be easier, and I mean a lot easier.

The floor staff work hard, very hard, and generally for a lot less than you will be earning. You will need to make sure they like you and are behind you before you try to implement these ideas - walking in on the first night and suggesting them, will get their backs up and put you in a negative position.

Once you have a good rapport with the staff you will be able to suggest some ideas that you can implement that will bring you together as a team rather than 'us and them'.

The Host with the Most.

When the customers enter the restaurant they are normally met by either a Maître de, or a host/hostess, or a sign that says "Wait here to be seated". The staff member who meets and greets can let the customer know that tonight is "Magic Night" and there is a table magician in attendance. They can tell the customer that they will personally ask the magician to visit their table (putting them in a good position with the customer), or warn you off if they say they are not interested.

The Waiter's suggestion.

If there is no main host then the waiter/waitress who takes the order can do the above instead.

This can work in their favour, as a good performance from you can lead to a nice tip for them. In F&B's some of the waiters will actually call over to me and ask me to visit their customers next - a nice display that shows the rest of the restaurant that you are not only in demand, but you must be worth watching too.

The Magician's Apprentice.

The floor staff are normally very busy, but if you get a quiet moment and you want to inject a little fun into the show then using a staff member can be an excellent way to do this.

Idea 1

Have the waiter bring an envelope to the table at a designated signal, this could include a duplicate card or card prediction, etc.

This is limited only by your imagination.

Idea 2

This one takes a little more set up but in the right venue, can be amazing, Give each of the floor staff 6 duplicate cards in order, have them place them in their breast pocket and at any time you call out, "What's the chosen card?" all the staff members who are able to at that time, can reach in and bring out the front card and show it to the whole room, then place the card at the back of the pile so the next force card is at the front ready to be brought into view.

Idea 3

If you use a signed card, at the end of the routine as you leave the table take the card with you. Do not draw attention to this, just pick it up and put it in the pack and as you wish them goodbye slip the cards into your pocket. Go to the waiter and ask them to deliver the card when they take the bill, along with one of your business cards. This does not sound like much at all, but it gets a good laugh at the end of the meal. This simple action has generated a lot of work for me. When I am at their event, a lot of clients will misremember the story and say that the waiter brought the card to their table whilst I am still stood there, making me even better than I am.

Remember the staff are busy, and you are there to complement them, not harass them into being in a certain spot at a certain time.

When used correctly, these techniques will build a bond between you and the staff, and give the customers an experience they would not normally get.

Tips.

I have mentioned elsewhere in the book that I do not generally accept tips.

This is not always the case and depends on the restaurant and on the clientèle, in some places I do accept tips. Therefore, I wanted to share a few ways to help increase the tips you get.

I find that I get more tips when I am not chasing them. If you work hard and present well, then you will get tipped; but if you distract yourself, and get addicted to the idea of more money then you will end up performing badly - this will affect your relationship with the venue as well. Keep focused, do your job, do it well and the tips will happen.

However there are some methods to getting more tips

The trick with the money

Borrow a small note note and use it in a trick, note in lemon, bill switch or the like. At the end of the effect the spectator may be inclined to let you keep it. This method reaped me a lot of tips when I worked on the cruise ships in Finland.

The money transfer

Whilst you are at the table, take some notes and coins from one pocket and transfer it into another pocket. You are not saying you want a tip, it suggests others have already tipped and may encourage them to follow suit.

These following methods I am not to keen on, to me they look like begging.

Funny Badge

The performer uses a funny badge that implies they should tip.

The Comedy Card

During a card effect it says on one of the cards "Please tip" or similar.

The tips jar

Not very subtle but you have a jar with a few notes and a few coins in, on the side of the jar is a white label saying "Tips". When the customers see this, they know they can tip and that others have already tipped, so may feel inclined to do so too.

The money clip

Another not very subtle way to show you can accept tips. It works the same as the above method, but does not take up as much room; also, by folding the note in half and clipping it, it makes it look like there is twice as much money in the pile.

Whatever method you go for, remember to be polite, respectful and remember that you are getting paid a fee, regardless of how much it is - it is a fee you have agreed. Any tips are a bonus, and are not compulsory, every customer has the right to tip or not to tip, but you have to treat them all the same and be professional.

Working in the Restaurant.

Sometimes during your session the restaurant may go quiet; this will happen and you want to show that even though the venue is not busy, you still are. You could entertain the staff if all the customers are eating, but if there are people sat waiting I would recommend switching your style of performance from normal work mode, to relaxed mode.

Spend longer at the tables, chat with the customers and build a bond, make them laugh and pay them some extra attention. When the manager comes out and sees all the staff standing in the corner, or at the bar, but sees you in the middle of the restaurant engaging the customers, he will see his investment in you was a worthwhile decision.

Children.

Entertaining children can be a very scary prospect if you have never done it before.

I would suggest you stay away from the slapstick style approach of a children's entertainer. I am not saying there is anything wrong with it in a children's show, but in this environment it is completely out of place. I talk to the children like they are adults, I do not condescend or put on silly voices, instead I talk normally to them and perform for the group. I **do not** perform just for the children. This does a number of things, including not alienating the rest of the table or setting myself up for just working tables with children.

The tricks I do at these tables: Sponge Balls, TT and Silk, Coin Vanish are simple but effective; they are good for everyone to watch - from toddlers to grandparents.

Do not underestimate the power of the magic in a simple sponge ball routine.

Work the group as a whole, do not just use the children, use the adults too; bring them all into the effect and you will make a massive positive impression that is undeniable and long lasting.

The Bar Area.

Some restaurants have a bar area, and during the busiest times I will switch between the restaurant floor and the bar area.

This enables me to work away from the normal constrictions of the restaurant. I can spend more time with people (as I do not have to move for food); I can use the bar surface to do table top effects that I would not be able to use around the tables.

Even though I only really work around the tables after the order has been taken but before the food arrives, if I work in the bar area it looks like I am helping by not holding up the diners, thus getting the tables cleared sooner.

Regular and Repeat Customers.

These can be the restaurant magicians greatest ally or biggest nuisance. The regular customer will have the ear of the manager or owner, so you need to get these people on side, show them something new every time they come in, be their best mate: teach them a simple card trick or coin trick. They will talk to the owner/manager and will praise you right up the kazoo.

Having repeat customers is great, it keeps you on your toes and can be an influence to change your set. I never do the same tricks table to table, I carry a certain number on me, but like the freedom to be able to do what I feel is best rather than a pre-prepared set that never deviates.

Breaks.

I find that during the night, there are times when you can

naturally take a break. This for me is straight after a busy period while waiting for the tables tables to clear for the next sitting. You do not want to be in the way or delay this process, so it is a perfect time to take 5 minutes. Taking a break every 20 minutes will annoy the staff and management and make you look lazy.

Do not take too many or take too long, or you will end up on a permanent break!

Here are some hints and tips that will make an impression with both staff and customers; they are ideas that will make life a lot easier for you when working:

- Avoid any tricks that require table space, the table top is the customer's personal space and is best avoided.

- All effects need to be instant reset or at most 5 second reset. The manager will not like it if you have to disappear after every table.

- Enjoy and have fun. Do not shy away from loud tables - be seen to be creating an atmosphere.

- Be smart but do not overdress - complement the venue. Overdressing may put people off watching you.

- Avoid dressing like a children's entertainer, silly waistcoats or card ties will make you look amateur and cheapen what you do and the restaurant you are working in.

- Do not forget that you are part of a team, and as such customers may assume they can ask you to get drinks or take orders. Smile, say that you will get a server to attend them and go get a server. Remember the smile is important.

- Smile. Never underestimate the power of a smile.

- Remember to watch where you stand and be aware hat other tables are watching too: this means angles become an issue. Also, remember which effects you have done nearby, as they may have already seen the effect when you did it across from them. Do not assume that just because they are eating at another table, that they are not watching you.
- Vary your Act. Be sure to add new effects to your act so repeat customers always get something new and fresh.
- I normally start my set after the order has been taken, this is the longest time between courses. If the food comes whilst you are still working, finish quick and move on to the next table.
- Be prepared for them to say NO.
- Be prepared for those that say no to call you back later in the session.
- Have fun and enjoy it, working in a restaurant is one of the most fun and fulfilling venues you will work. Everything is more relaxed and informal. Make friends, build contacts and try out new material.

The Business in Show-Business.

It always amazes me, the number of magicians who do not understand the meaning of that simple statement.

When I worked with Rodney James Piper in Spain, at the beginning of the new season the first lessons we taught the entertainments team was that we are in SHOW-BUSINESS.

A lot of people assume, wrongly, that because the word SHOW comes first, that is the most important part; however, this is not the case.

If you only take one thing from this book then let it be this:
Without the business, there can be no show.

When you work in a venue, restaurant or otherwise, you are a supplier. This is the category you will be listed under when you invoice the company, and how the higher-ups will refer to you in meetings: it is your status within the company.

You supply a service to the company, when the area manager comes to the venue and you are there, you will probably be introduced to them thus:
"This is Wayne, he is one of our suppliers, he is the Magician".

Supplier first, Magician second. This is because, believe it or not, the Company does not look at you as a magician, it looks at you as a service supplier. You come under the same category as the company that supplies the beer, soft drinks and toilet cleaning equipment.

As stated before, you are working as part of a business, and with this in mind, it is important to remember that the management will be looking for a ROI from you.

Return On Investment (ROI)

Business 101. There is no company in the world that pays

out money without expecting a return on that investment. Some companies will expect a service, for example if you pay a plumber £x to fix your sink, then you expect the sink to be fixed. Some companies will expect a ROI in the shape of value. The restaurant will want something in-between.

Almost all the restaurants I work for want between 3/1 - 5/1 ROI, which means for every £1 they pay me, they need to make between £3 - £5 back.

Now this seems like it is adding a lot of pressure to you - how can you be responsible for that kind of income to the restaurant?

Believe it or not, this is not as bleak as it sounds. All you have to do to achieve, or help to achieve this, is be good at your job and tell everyone about what you are doing.

That is a slightly over simplified answer, but essentially it is correct.

Almost every restaurant will book you for the busy period (we will look at which nights are the best and the worst elsewhere in the book). This means you are already in a position to be seen to be an asset. In addition to assisting the venue by entertaining customers waiting to be seated in the bar area, or when there is a small delay in the kitchen, make sure you encourage repeat business: tell the customers when you will be back and tell them to book early so they can see you again. I get the customers to write a comment on the restaurant Facebook page too - this is direct feedback to the management.

Increasing your value.

The management will increase your net value to the restaurant every time you are mentioned:

- When someone calls up and books a table and mentions you.
- When customers are leaving and thank the staff and say how excellent you are.
- When customers write on the restaurant's social media page and say how you made the evening perfect.
- When you leave a table, and they are clapping and cheering.
- When a table asks the waiting staff to get you to go back to the table.

These things all amount to your value as an asset. This means that even when the restaurant is quieter than normal or is having a slow night, YOU can still maintain a HIGH value by being the one who provides.

In the first few months I am working a new restaurant I will make sure that when a problem arises, I am in place to help deal with it. This means letting the floor staff know that if they have a awkward customer or if there is a delay in the kitchen, they can send me over to the table.

If people are waiting at the bar, children are crying, or there are big groups, then I go over. Bigger groups require a little longer so the kitchen has a chance to prepare all the food.

Be seen to be part of the team, show the staff some tricks when they are not working or when they are on a break. Show the staff that you are a team player and do not think yourself above them.

Be loyal to the hand that feeds you. If someone starts complaining, do not get involved or be seen to agree with them. The complaining customer would love to be able to say,

"The food was disgusting, even the magician said it looked bad".

This will lead very quickly to the end of your last ever session in the restaurant.

Everything that happens in the restaurant should flow smoothly in accordance with each other, the floor staff, the manager, the general manager, the kitchen staff, the cleaners, and you.

You need to flow with the staff and become part of the restaurant. If you can do this and become part of the symbiotic circle, then you become indispensable to the restaurant. Think about that for a moment. Think about being so important to the restaurant that you could have regular work for years. Think about being so important to the restaurant, that in their eyes, they can not be without you.

- Watch the management.
- Watch the staff.
- Learn the business.
- Become part of the team.
- Work.

The management wants to add value to the service they are providing. You are in a unique position to offer something different. Something that is more than a voucher they will probably lose. Something they will take away and talk about. Something that will encourage repeat custom and generate more revenue.

One of my favourite business quotes, "*To be successful, you have to have your heart in your business, and your business in your heart.*" *Sir Thomas Watson.*

Residency vs Gig.

For the sake of completion I wanted to add a chapter that made reference to the main differences between a residency and a one-off gig.

Obviously the residency is a long-term commitment. This means you will need to have a large selection of effects, and be able to adapt to changing situations. You will be part of a bigger team as opposed to being a stand alone act.

The main difference is the money. The fee you normally command is likely to be miles away from the fee the restaurant wants to pay, you may get lucky and be able to pull in a decent amount; however, most of the time you will be taking a cut in short-term financial gratification. This does not mean that you will be losing out in the long-term.

Choosing the right times to work, being seen by a good number of people and handing out business cards, etc. means you can turn it into an advertising opportunity.

There are a large number of perks to working a residency. One major advantage is you will see customers again and again, especially the regulars. This means you can build relationships with people that can provide a source of income for years.

I use all my residencies as a form of marketing and as a great place to try out new material.

Another difference is that you can fill your diary on nights when normally you would not be working. A Tuesday night is not normally a busy night for me, so I can fill it with a restaurant.

Building a good relationship with the management also gives me a lot of freedom. I try and keep my residencies to non-peak nights, but on occasion it allows me to take a

Friday or Saturday night if I do not have anything else booked in.

Although I am not getting my normal fee, I still see an income and it is an opportunity to be seen, and therefore a possible chance to generate more work. Better this than sitting at home earning nothing.

Another big difference between a residency and a gig is the ability to break in new material, this has been mentioned elsewhere in the book, but do not overlook it.

Learn the method and bash out a simple routine, then put it to work at the restaurant. Performance has always been the best rehearsal and you have the opportunity to really work it. By the time you finish the session, you should have an effect that is either set and polished or well on its way to being so.

Keeping The Gig.

So you have contacted the establishment, met the management and got the gig, the contracts are signed and you are now a regular at the restaurant. You have established a relationship with the other staff and you now have a few regulars - a fan base of sorts.

So what do you do now? How do you keep the gig?

I am going to share some techniques that will generate honest positive feedback, and some that will be slightly less honest but very effective. Some of the ideas can only be used once, maybe twice, others you can use at every table. All have been, and continue to be, used by me at all my residencies.

The first few will be honest forms and ones you can use every session.

Ask for some applause.

I hate it when I am working at a gig with another magician and he starts asking the tables to clap him louder, its pathetic ego stroking and disrespectful to other performers working; however, in the restaurant, when it's just you and the customers - game on. At the end of your set at the table, as you are thanking the table, if they do not automatically start clapping, then let them know it's OK.

"Thanks guys, you have been great. Enjoy the rest of your meal and as I walk away, if you feel the urge to clap, I may get paid tonight! Cheers."

"Please keep all applause to a maximum."

"Cheers everyone, you have been a great table. Just so all the other tables know how much you have enjoyed the show, as I leave if you could, a small round of applause will tell them to watch too, or a standing ovation if you like!"

All lines should be said a little tongue in cheek, 99% of tables will be more than happy to comply - if you have done a good job that is.

Applause is a great form of feedback, not only does it tell the manager and other staff that you really are making an impression and building a fun atmosphere, it also tells other other tables who you are and what you are doing. This is an invaluable weapon in your arsenal for breaking the ice with new tables, etc.

Ask for feedback.

When I finish my set, I normally spend a few seconds at the table wishing them an enjoyable meal, and leave some of my business cards on the table for the group. Before I leave the table, I will turn to the table as a whole and I will say,

"Cheers guys, enjoy the rest of your meal. If you have enjoyed my magic please let your waiter know, or the manager, and I may see you here again next time you visit."

This is important as the manager will ask the waiting staff for any comments on your performance. Telling the customers to speak to the waiter will also mean that the customer will probably do this as they are giving a tip, this will cause an association between your performance and more money for the waiter; this puts you in an excellent position with the floor staff and will help build a relationship with them.

Ask for more feedback.

This idea is very similar to the last one; however, this time you are going to ask them to make a comment on your Facebook page or Twitter or other social media site. Again, this is a great technique as you will get a contact from them, and you can share/re-tweet the comment onto the page of the restaurant, so the management see it too. A lot of times they do this, they will also write on their wall automatically.

These ideas are a little less honest but are very effective, do not overlook these, it's only a small deception.

A friend indeed.

You need a friend who is coming to the restaurant on the night you will be there. This is simple and very effective, all they need to do is phone up and book a table, and ask if the magician they had heard about was going to be there. That is it: simple but deadly. However, the manager will hear about it and will be aware that the reputation of having a magician is working.

The Booking.

This idea, when used, is one of the most effective techniques you can use, I would recommend that you only use it once, more than that and you run the risk of being caught out, which will not only destroy your reputation, but probably cost you the gig as well.

I cannot remember who it was who shared this goldmine of an idea with me, but he will forever have my thanks: the set-up is the same as before, all you need is a friend who is coming to the restaurant on the night you will be there. Let's assume you're working on Saturday 6pm – 8pm. The importance of these logistics will become clear in a moment.

You need your friend to call the restaurant to book at a table

(Host) *"Good evening, this is XX restaurant, how can I help?"*

(Friend) *"Good evening, I was hoping to book a table for 4 people on FRIDAY night please"*

(Host) *"No problem"*

(Friend) *"I understand you have a magician who works in the restaurant, could I ask that he comes to our table at some point please?"*

(Host) *"Yes that is correct, unfortunately he is not working Friday. He is working Saturday however"*

(Friend) *"Really? Saturday, hold on one second"*

(Friend holding phone away as if speaking to wife/partner, etc.) *"The magician is not there Friday, he is there Saturday though"*

The friend should now wait a few seconds as if talking to someone, (unless his wife is there and will play along).

(Friend) *"Can we change our table to Saturday night please".*

This is a great way to build a reputation with the manager. From his point of view the customer has enquired about you, asked for a performance and CHANGED his plans for dinner to suit you. WOW! you must be awesome.

I use this technique ONCE at each restaurant, normally after I have been there a few months, just to kick the manager into place and remind them just how awesome I am.

The, not so, anonymous customer.

If you have any friends coming to the restaurant, get them to pass on a comment, or speak to the manager. I once had a mate go up to the bar (where the manager happened to be stood watching the room) and order a beer. He then casually turned to the manager and just commented,

"That magician is awesome, have you seen what he can do with a pack of cards, brilliant!", then he picked-up his beer and walked away. To the manager this was amazing feedback. In his eyes, the customer had just made a random comment to a random member of staff, he did not know he was a manager (even though he did).

My mate also added a few words to the waiter, and on the restaurant Facebook page a few days later.

Keeping the gig, is not as hard as it sounds, if you deliver on the promises you make. Perform well and get feedback, you will become an investment the company will want to keep and utilise.

Publicity Material.

One of the main differences between a residency and a normal gig is the kind of publicity material I hand out.

When I perform at a wedding or trade show I have sophisticated looking clear-plastic cards with white lettering: they look good, and bring in a lot of work. However, they do cost a bit more, so I want to make sure I only use them on the shows that will generate a good fee.

When I perform at a restaurant I can give out normal card business cards by the dozen.

For my restaurants here is my business card:

The QR Code goes to my homepage and it has all the

relevant information on the front. The back of the card is blank so I can use it for predictions, etc.

I also have postcards that I give away at restaurants, although bigger than a business card they actually work for me 75% more than the cards do.

The actual pictures I use change with every new order of cards, just to keep them up to date.

This is my post card:

The front of the card has lots of pictures and all the relevant information; however, the back of this card is not blank. As it is a post card I designed the back like this:

The back of the card has some quotes, all the relevant

information again, and a picture of a post it note that I use for predictions, etc.

I will give these cards out around the tables, and also place a large stack on the desk at the front of the restaurant.

In some of the larger restaurants I work, such as Frankie and Benny's, I also have a pull up banner in between the bar and the front door, so people waiting for a table are looking at it and know that I am in the restaurant.

One of my smaller independent residencies also had a large banner made up that they display above the front window so anyone passing gets to see the advert.

This really works, I get a lot of positive feedback from people who see it.

This also shows a great level of commitment to each other, and 4 years later I am still working at this restaurant, and have indeed made many invaluable contacts and friendships that continue to bring me business, year after year.

Publicity material is one of the best tools we have, alongside a good website and being a good performer.

Other things I have used as give-a-ways will be listed below:

Plastic wrist bands (similar to charity bands)

http://www.thewrist-band.co.uk/

I have it printed with my website and with a card prediction.

These are a great give-a-way and the company I get them on offers such as "Buy 100 get 100 free", making them even more cost-effective.

Flyers – Brochures – Magnets - Poker chips

http://www.premierpokerchips.com/

Personalised Playing Cards

http://www.ivorygraphics.co.uk/bridge-playing-cards.asp?
gclid=CI7wutragrsCFacSwwodPD4ANg

These are great to use, slip one into your normal deck and force the card for a great impromptu effect with your business "Card"

www.Fiverr.com

Great for getting personalised, bespoke items, such as cartoons, intro videos, etc.

All these have been met with different degrees of success.

Talking Points.

One the things that has kept me working, and generated more work within the restaurant industry is that I realised the customer's need to continue to be amazed even after I leave the table, and if possible, have them thinking about me every time they visit the venue.

So how do you do this? How do you create a talking point?

My first residency was at Frankie and Benny's. Over a period of time I plastered the ceiling with approximately 500 signed playing cards:

- People coming into the restaurant see the cards and ask about them.
- The customers who signed the cards will always look for their card when they revisit the venue.
- Customers will ask if they can add a card to the collection.

A talking point has been created.

Any effect that leaves either a enduring memory or souvenir will become a talking point. Do not underestimate the power of a souvenir as a talking point.

- A signed card that the spectator keeps can be a powerful reminder, I get booked by clients who have kept their card in their wallet for years.
- A Card on the ceiling.
- A solid fork that has been bent out of shape

- A pack of cards sealed inside a bottle is an amazing

piece of magical art. Get one and give it to the restaurant to place behind the bar on display, put a business card next to it or a sign announcing there is a close-up magician.

- These bottles can be purchased from a good friend of mine named Chris Harding, his website is www.cardsinabottle.co.uk Each bottle is hand made by Chris and is beautiful beyond compare.

The whole concept of a talking point is to encourage the customer to remember what has happened, and to show new customers what happens in the venue.

Public Liability Insurance.

If you perform for the public in any setting: at home, in the garden, children's shows, family magic, stage, restaurants, weddings etc, then you NEED to be covered by P.L.I.

In some cases this will be a legal requirement.

Most independent insurance companies will offer a minimum cover of £5 million. Policies range in price, so it is worth spending an afternoon doing some research into which best fits your budget and requirements.

What is Public Liability Insurance?

Public liability insurance provides cover in the event that a member of the public is accidentally injured and your business is found to be liable. The cover will also protect you if you damage a member of the public's property whilst working at their home.

If your business has made a mistake which leads to an incident causing damage to a customer or their property it's likely that this will result in a public liability claim. Claims for trips, slips and falls are among the most common type of public liability claims.

The cost of legal fees and expenses is all included for both defending the claim and paying out should you be found to be at fault. Public liability will only cover third party damages and does not include injuries to employees. This is dealt with through employer's liability insurance.

You or your business will have to be found at fault for a

customer to receive compensation through your public
liability insurance policy.

Equity:

I use Equity to provide my P.L.I.

http://www.equity.org.uk/home/ There are a number of advantages to
using Equity, not only do I get £10 million cover but I also
get the full legal support, name support, etc.

I have included a list of the complete benefits of being an
Equity member at the end of the chapter.

Why do I need Public Liability Insurance?

Imagine you break something in a customer's house, or
knock a table at a wedding and spill red wine over the
bride's dress, lose a ring you have borrowed or someone
gets hurt whilst helping you with an effect.

close-up or on stage anything can happen, are you
prepared for the repair or legal costs? Can you afford the
compensation for a £1,700 wedding dress?

Benefits of being an Equity Member.

Equity membership brings with it a range of benefits

including representation, advice, relevant services and other

things of practical value that are aimed at supporting

members throughout their career:

Spend an evening reviewing different options and checking

out as many companies as you can.

Risk Assessment.

My own personal risk assessment was constructed by doing a google search of "Risk Assessment" and reading through a lot of pages, to choose the bits that would be relevant to what I do.

This chapter is not just for restaurant work, it will detail exactly what a risk assessment is and you will be able to take what you need when putting together a risk assessment if required.

This chapter was written with the kind consent from some of my sources, they have been credited where applicable.

What is a risk assessment?

A risk assessment is an examination of what, in the process of an event, could cause harm to people. The aim is to identify any hazards, decide the probability of the accident occurring and to decide what (if anything) should be done to reduce the risks or effects.

Hazard: anything that can cause harm (e.g. hot lights, electrically unsafe equipment)

Risk: the chance that somebody will be harmed by the hazard

When you first start to work for a company, restaurant or otherwise you may be asked to fill out a risk assessment.

This may be the first time you have had to do this.

Whilst researching this chapter I found this on the website of the Fellowship of Christian Magicians (http://www.fcmuk.org/freebies/risk.htm), and they have very gracefully allowed me to reproduce their text as follows:

Security of the audience and staff in and out of the building or area

The audience should be able to enter and exit the performance area in an orderly manner without risk of injury. There should be no obstructions or obstacles to impede their exit. All exits and walk ways must be clearly illuminated and signposted. This is particularly important in the event of emergency evacuation of the area.

Capacity of the hall, theatre or place of presentation

The place where the entertainment is to take place must be capable of holding the number of people who have been sold tickets. Careful control is needed on all entry and exit points, to ensure that only people with tickets are admitted to the area. All places of entertainment should have a fire certificate which should state the maximum number of people allowed in the building at any one time.

Electrical equipment

Lighting, amplification and other electrical equipment either belonging to the building or to the performer should have a current test certificate which states that at the time of testing it was safe and fit for use.

Falling objects

Lighting rigs and other properties such as PA speakers, scenery and aerial props should be correctly secured and where possible should have additional safety chains attached just in case they become detached from their mounting brackets or rigs. This will prevent them falling on people and will give extra time for the area to be evacuated.

Medical Emergency

In the case of a medical emergency the medical team should be able to easily reach the casualty to treat them or remove them for treatment elsewhere.

Magicians additional risks

All magicians are to have up to date public liability insurance (Minimum £5million). Some of the things which magicians can do which can injure or cause damage are listed below

Cuts from sharp objects

Even simple playing cards can cause injury if incorrectly used. A playing card spun at high speed can inflict a serious cut and could blind somebody if it hits them in the eye. Blades and other sharp objects used in magic props and tricks can also cause serious injury.

Falling

Some illusions involve the performer or assistants being either suspended or above ground height. There is therefore always the risk of falling causing injury to themselves and whoever they land on.

Poison

Some magical illusions use toxic chemicals in their presentation. Extreme care must be exercised in their storage, handling, use and disposal. A record should be kept of what these chemicals are in case there is an accident so that the emergency people will know what treatment is required.

Toxic fumes caused by chemical reactions or combustion could also cause choking or respiratory problems in a confined area.

Choke hazards

Great care should be exercised if small prizes or other objects are handed out to children as they could cause choking if swallowed. Some illusions can also cause a choke hazard to the performer or their assistant if they go wrong. An escape procedure for these particular effects should be discussed with the performer before they are allowed to present them.

Allergies

More and more people these days are developing allergies to various foods and other substances. Lots of magicians and other entertainers use balloons in their acts. Some people have an allergy to latex so if they are handed a balloon by the performer it could cause them problems.

Fire

Various magical effects employ fire. Some of these may be very small such as an appearing lighted candle but a naked flame is present nonetheless. Care should therefore be taken that the effects are presented well away from any flammable materials and fire/smoke detectors. If a sprinkler system is set off accidentally by a simple fire effect it could cause a lot of water damage from the sprinkler system.

Projectiles

Items such as streamers and confetti can be projected by compressed gases, springs, elastics, pneumatics and explosions. Care needs to be exercised to ensure that the projectiles do not hit anybody.

Explosions

As with fire effects, extreme care should be taken in the use of pyrotechnics. Only commercial pyrotechnics should be used and only under a strict safety code of operation.

Home made explosives and pyrotechnics should never be used.
Explosions and flashes can also be obtained from clouds of fine powder ignited by a spark or a flame. Extreme care needs to be taken in their use.

Flooding

Some illusions employ large amounts of liquid. If the container is ruptured it could cause flooding, injury and property damage.

Suffocation

Some magical effects especially escape routines could cause suffocation to the performer or their assistant if they go wrong. This is either through the chest being restricted or confinement in an airtight container. An emergency escape procedure should be arranged with the performer prior to allowing the effect to be performed.

Firearms

Effects involving firearms of any description are dangerous. Blank cartridges can injure or kill when they detonate if they are wrongly used. A loaded firearm can also detonate if it is dropped onto the floor.

Criminal Records

It is very important especially when working with children and young people that the entertainer has been properly checked for working with children and young people and that their CRB certificate is clear and up to date.

Not all of this is relevant to the close-up/restaurant magician; however, it is information that may be useful and shows the level of information required in some venues.

The risk assessment may be a lot shorter than this for a residency but no less important.

You will need to evaluate the whole of your act, every trick, prop and piece of equipment you use.

Remember that some venues will not book you if they see items of danger, and be prepared for them to not allow fire or flash items.

Why assess risk?

The point of a risk assessment is NOT to eliminate all risk. It is to reduce risk to acceptable levels.

For example, by doing a risk assessment, you may find that a show requires more fire extinguishers than in the venue or that some need to be moved to better locations. The risk assessment is there to open your eyes to potential dangers, to plan how to prevent problems before they occur, and to reduce the effects of accidents.

Many people (in the Student's Union, the University and Industry) require risk assessments. It an ability that you almost certainly will use in future life and in some instances, is required by law.

It's not complicated!

Life is unpredictable, and so identifying absolutely everything that could go wrong is unnecessary. You could look at the chance of a meteorite crashing into the venue - but there wouldn't be much point!

Breaking every danger into its precise parts isn't needed; e.g. specifying hazards on each and every type of light is just going to extremes. In this instance you would usually state the hazard as a defective light which could cause injury. A way to reduce the risk would be to make sure all lights have been electrically tested (PAT test), ensure all lights have effective hook clamps and safety wires, and visually check each light as it is rigged.

Who should do it?

There is no specified person who should carry out a risk assessment, but the event manager should ensure that it is done. If you are in any doubt, please ask the Backstage Safety Officer for help.

What do I do with it?

As part of a risk assessment, you will produce a series of measures that would reduce the risk or effect of the hazard. By ensuring that you actually do this, the safety of everybody is improved.

Make sure everyone is aware of it: you're not the only one in danger. If people don't know that certain things need to be done, then they won't do them and the entire process is a waste of time.
If situations change, then the risk assessment will need to be reviewed to ensure that it actually matches up with what's happening at your event.

DOING A RISK ASSESSMENT

Identify hazards

Have a walk around the venue, look at the lighting plan, work out where all the set is going to go. Have a think about the timetable, are you transporting anything? Any heavy lifting? Any unusual equipment? What could go wrong?
A method that works well is to think through the event in chronological order. So for a show:

- Collection of equipment: any heavy lifting?
- Rehearsals/Performance: Burns? Fire? Ear damage? Strobes? Slipping? e.g. Hazard of hot light causing person to burn hands.

Decide who might be harmed and by how much
In Backstage work, the people involved usually fall into one or more of three categories: crew, cast/performers and public. It should also be divided into numbers of people; individual, small or large.
The severity of the harm is split into

- minor: small cut/burn/bruise
- major: severe cut/burn/bruise
- fatality: you kill someone

It is common to give the severity as a range of categories,

e.g. Individual crew member burns hands on hot light during get out with severity minor-major.

Evaluate risks

Is the chances of this hazard high, medium or low? e.g. Depending on the competence of the crew, the chances of this happening is probably medium.

Decide on precautions

What needs to be done to reduce the chances of the accident occurring? Can anything be done to reduce the effects of an accident?

- Try a less risky option.
- Prevent access to the hazard.
- Organise work to reduce exposure to the hazard.
- Issue personal protective equipment.
- Provide equipment & facilities for accident occurring.

Do it!

Write it out, make people aware of it and ensure that the precautions are carried out.

Go For It.

Not many people know that when you write a book you actually end up writing 2 books, sometimes 3 or 4 books. You start with an idea and then comes the rewrite, and the 2nd rewrite and so on. The original book I wrote on this subject is a shadow compared to the book you now hold.

I am very proud of what I have achieved in my years as a magician. I never sought fame or fortune, rather I wanted to make a living. I wanted to be comfortable in my chosen profession and be able to support my family. I never realised that restaurant magic would become a major part of what I do.

I love working in restaurants. I love the ambience and the pressure, and the knowledge that I am contributing to someone's evening on a very personal level. When I first started working in restaurants I quickly saw how busy I would become. I knew that I would have to completely change my work habits, and rethink the structure of what I do in order to accommodate what would become a major source of income.

I also love that I get to try out ideas, and new effects on a friendly crowd, before putting them into my main show repertoire - giving me the opportunity to fine tune in front of an audience rather than just in front of a mirror.

Take the information in this book and use it, adapt it, personalise it and make it work for you. I hope if nothing else the one thing you take from this book is my passion for what I do.

I would like to end the book with a quote that inspires me every day: it's my mantra, my belief.

Once in an interview I was told that when on stage I looked like I was having as much fun as the audience, I told them, "I know you cannot please all the people all the time, however I go on stage with the mindset that I will have a good time, and rather than try and please everyone, I will just enjoy what I do and if the audience would like to join me, it will be a hell of a ride".

Thank you again for buying this book, I hope you get as much out of reading it as I have writing it, and please look out for the next book in the "Wayne Goodman Definitive" series.

Wayne Goodman
January 2014

www.waynegoodman.co.uk